Rock Snot, Cane Toads and Other Aliens

Written by Nancy O'Connor
Series Consultant: Linda Hoyt

WorldWise
Content-based Learning

Contents

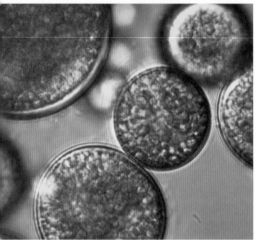

Introduction

Did you know we are being invaded by crabs? Oysters? And rock snot? These **alien** invaders don't come from outer space. Blasters and light sabres won't work on these creatures. But it costs millions of dollars every year to fight them.

These **invasive species** are plants, **algae** and animals. They go places they don't belong and crowd out **native** plants and animals. Consequently, these invaders eventually take over and smother, choke, poison or eat the natives. This sounds like the plot of a movie, doesn't it?

Humans often introduce alien life forms to new environments, but nature can be responsible, too. Even the ocean can play a role in helping an invasive species hitchhike to a new home. Scientists found ocean-going rubbish along the west coast of the United States that had floated across the Pacific after Japan's tsunami in 2011. Millions of creatures – mussels, oysters, starfish, crabs and fish – travelled almost 8,000 kilometres on this rubbish.

Introducing a species into an **ecosystem** where it doesn't belong can bring disaster. These alien invaders are a global problem, and researchers everywhere are trying to figure out how to fight them.

Chapter 1

Plant and algae predators

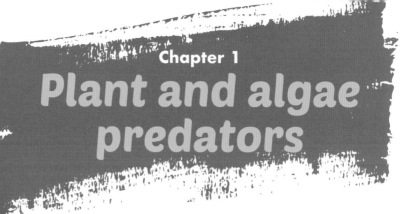

Buffel grass

Buffel grass is a type of weed **native** to Africa and the Middle East. It was first introduced into Australia in the 1920s as food for livestock. Farmers knew it was drought resistant, so they hoped it would grow well in the dry outback areas of northern and central Australia. It did – it grew too well!

Therefore, buffel grass is a big problem. It has begun to crowd out native plants of similar size. It competes for whatever water is available and can weaken and kill larger desert plants. The grass spreads even in very dry years. Its dense roots prevent the seeds of native plants from **germinating**.

Buffel grass

Buffel grass on the edge of northern Simpson Desert, southwest Queensland, Australia

But one of the greatest dangers of buffel grass is how **flammable** it is. Buffel grass burns so fiercely, flames can spread across an area the size of a football field in less than four minutes. Most plant fires burn at 300 to 400 degrees Celsius. Buffel grass burns at 700 to 750 degrees Celsius. And the effects of a fire like this can be devastating to the desert **ecosystem**.

In central Australia, where large areas are covered in buffel grass, bushfires are more frequent. When there is a buffel grass fire, nearly all the native plants in its path are killed and they won't grow back. They have no way to **regenerate**.

But what will grow back is the buffel grass. Its roots beneath the soil remain alive after fires, and it comes back as strongly as ever. If this **invasive** grass is not contained, it is possible that the plant diversity of the desert will be destroyed forever.

Buffel grass bushfires burn hot and fast.

7

The plant can grow at the rate of 30 centimetres a day! That means the vine might completely cover you in four or five days.

Kudzu

Kudzu is a vine with purple flowers that is a member of the pea family. It has many uses, such as animal feed, medicine and tea. The **fibre** from the plant can be woven into baskets, clothing and paper. All that sounds good, doesn't it? But kudzu is listed amongst the world's most **invasive** alien **species**.

Kudzu was introduced in the southern United States in the late 1800s, but it has since gone wild. If you left your bicycle leaning up against a back fence for a couple of days, you might never be able to find it again. Kudzu has even been known to cover abandoned cars and houses. In the United States, it covers an area equal to 50,000 football fields every year. No wonder some people call it "the vine that ate the South!"

Goats graze on kudzu

How are people fighting this invasive plant? Farmers graze their goats on kudzu plants. Sometimes it is burned or mowed down with machines. Plant poisons can be used on the roots to try to kill it. What once was a wonder plant has become a terrible pest.

Think like an environmentalist ...

The flowering plant Lantana is native to South America. It was brought to Australia as a garden plant in about 1841. It quickly spread, and within 20 years was established in the wild. Today, it covers four million hectares of eastern Australia and is costly to control. What can be done to stop plants from accidentally entering another country?

Rock snot

Rock snot's full name is *Didymosphenia geminate* or *Didymo*. This gross-sounding plant may look like a water weed, but it is a form of **microscopic algae**. The invasive algae form brown mats that can grow 20 centimetres thick in streambeds and lakes. Rock snot threatens water habitats, recreational areas, and other native plant and animal life.

Native to northern North America and Europe, rock snot has rapidly expanded its range to Australia, New Zealand and South America, where it is considered an invasive species.

Rock snot

Usually, this plant is found in cool, clear water. Rivers are particularly at risk. How do you know if you've found some rock snot in a stream? It is tan, brown or white, and as it ripples in the stream, it can look like stringy pieces of toilet paper. When you touch it, it feels more like wet wool than slimy snot. It is also tough, rather than flimsy, and doesn't break apart when rubbed between your fingers.

What sorts of problems does this invader cause? Rock snot can grow on the bottom of both flowing and still bodies of water. The algae choke out many of the other creatures that usually live there. That means less food for the trout and other fish in the area.

Unfortunately, people can accidentally spread rock snot from one body of water to another. It clings, unseen, to boots, boats, clothing and fishing equipment. To prevent the spread of rock snot, people should wash their boats and gear using hot water with soap, bleach and salt. They can also freeze their gear and clothing until everything is frozen solid and completely dry. Only then can people be certain any rock snot clinging to the items has died.

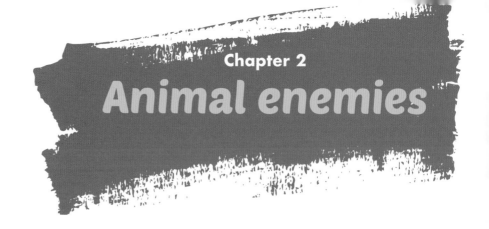

Cane toads

Cane toads were brought to Australia in 1935 to help control a beetle that was damaging the sugarcane crops. One hundred toads came in two suitcases, carried from the cane fields of Puerto Rico. Just as with the kudzu plant, this creature was introduced into the country on purpose. But the toads quickly multiplied, and today there are estimated to be over 1.5 billion in Australia. The largest one on record weighed almost two and a half kilograms.

What problems have the **alien** cane toads caused? They spread diseases to **native** animals. They also have poison glands along their backs. The **toxin** is so powerful, it can cause a heart attack in humans or their pets if they come in contact with it.

The Australian marsupial known as the Northern spotted quoll, about the size of a cat, is now on the endangered list because so many have died from eating cane toads.

Scientists at Kakadu National Park are trying to train quolls not to eat the toads. Captive quolls were fed small, dead cane toads that were injected with a chemical causing nausea. The toads were too small to kill the quolls. If the quolls could learn that toads made them sick, the scientists hoped they would avoid them. Before the "toad-smart" quolls were released back into the wild, they were fitted with tracking devices.

A cane toad

A Northern spotted quoll

The experiment has been a success! The scientists have found these "toad-smart" quolls are living five times longer than untrained ones. The researchers now hope these quolls will teach their babies to eat other things, like insects, birds and lizards.

The cane toads in Australia have developed longer legs over the time they have been there. That means they can hop faster and further. They are now spreading across the continent at the rate of 65 kilometres a year. Besides threatening native animal life, the cane toads never did solve the sugarcane beetle problem. Scientists failed to consider one small but important thing. The toads couldn't climb the tall sugarcane stalks to reach the beetles!

Did you know?

Speaking of longer legs, just like the cane toad, another creature has gotten taller to avoid alien predators. Over the last 70 years, lizards in Texas in the United States have grown longer legs so they can run faster when threatened by fire ants.

A swarm of fire ants

Fire ants swarm over and kill their prey.

Fire ants

Have you ever felt the burning, blistering sting of a fire ant? This insect is another **invasive species**. Red fire ants are very common in Australia, China, Taiwan and the southern United States. They feed mostly on plants and seeds, but they also eat other insects, birds, amphibians and reptiles.

They are aggressive insects and have been known to kill small animals, even baby calves. The fire ants swarm over their prey and sting them thousands of times. The toxin in their stings can be deadly to people, too.

Fire ants build nests on riverbanks, near ponds, in watered lawns and along highway shoulders. They have an amazing talent. When there is heavy rain and water begins to flood the tunnels of their nest, they grab their babies and run for it! Fire ants have waxy bodies that allow them to **repel** water. They link their legs together and form a floating raft. The ants protect their queen by forming a mass around her, as well as all the eggs, **larvae** and **pupae**. As the ants float, they rotate, so that the underwater ants have their turn at the top to get air.

Fire ants form a floating raft on water.

Red fire ants are native to Brazil and Argentina. They were first detected in Australia in 2001. Where did these nasty creatures come from? Scientists believe the ants were on a ship from the southern United States, where they are well established.

They think that the fire ants first landed in the southern United States in the late 1920s, also by ship. As the ship was unloaded, dockworkers removed the dirt that was used for ballast in the hold of the ship. It was dumped at the port. Unknown to the dockworkers, fire ants were living in that dirt.

Burmese pythons

Burmese pythons, giant snakes native to Asia, became a problem in the state of Florida in the United States after 1992. Hurricane Andrew destroyed a reptile-breeding **facility**, and all its pythons slithered into the wild. Female pythons can lay dozens of eggs at a time. Scientists estimate that 100,000 Burmese pythons live in the Florida Everglades today. Some can grow longer than 12 metres. This invasive snake has no natural enemies.

Even though pythons are not poisonous, their rows of teeth are razor sharp. The Burmese python wraps itself around its prey, squeezes and suffocates it. The snake's jaw can unhinge, allowing it to swallow things that would seem far too big. The snake can swallow its prey whole – they can even strangle and eat alligators and deer. However, they usually eat birds and small mammals, taking the food normally eaten by panthers, alligators and other animals that live in the Everglades.

In recent years, hunters have been hired to kill or capture the pythons. They often use drones to locate the snakes among the thick trees and bushes. Hunters are allowed to sell any pythons they capture.

Find out more

The Burmese python is not the only unwelcome visitor to the Florida Everglades. There are over 30 types of fish, 40 types of reptiles, about 12 types of birds, and about 17 different mammals that do not belong there. Find out more about these introduced animals and what is being done to get them out of the Everglades.

Chapter 3

Damage to an ecosystem

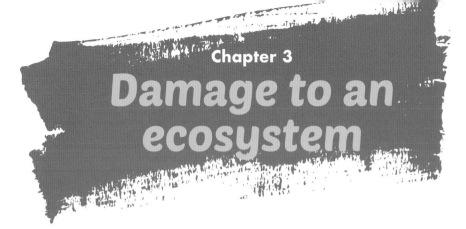

"The balance of nature" is the way creatures and plants live together in an **ecosystem**. Life is "balanced" when there is enough prey for the predators and enough plants and grasses for the insects and animals that need those things. But that "balance" can easily be tipped when a pet owner decides a snake has gotten too large or a ferret is too much trouble to care for, and then releases it into the wild. Those creatures can become **invasive species** and damage the ecosystem.

Animal invaders

Not all invasive creatures look creepy or are dangerous. Living things as ordinary as a rabbit or a fox can be an **alien** species.

Rabbits

A man named Thomas Austin imported 24 wild rabbits to Australia from England and released them for sport hunting.

The plague of rabbits in Australia in the 1930s

A fence built to keep out the rabbits

Because rabbits reproduce very quickly (one female can have 18 to 30 young per year), within a number of years, those 24 plant-eating rabbits multiplied, and soon there were no plants left.

The growth of the rabbit population in Australia was the fastest spread ever recorded of any mammal anywhere in the world. The country is an ideal habitat for rabbits. With mild winters, they are able to breed nearly year-round. Natural low vegetation provides them with shelter and food, and they have few predators. Rabbits eat both wild shrubs and farmers' crops. They search out tiny seedlings and the most tender, young plants to eat, so the plants don't grow and reproduce. By gnawing on tree bark, rabbits kill trees in orchards and forests. They have caused soil erosion problems by eating **native** plants, and their burrows can cause riverbanks and hillsides to collapse.

Rabbits burrowed under the fence!

To control the rabbits, people have tried hunting them, and they have even spread diseases known to kill rabbits. They have used explosives to destroy their burrows. Some people built fences across wide stretches of Australia to keep out the rabbits. Nothing has been very effective.

19

Foxes

The red foxes were also introduced for sport hunting, and they multiplied quickly, too. Today, there are an estimated seven and a half million foxes in Australia. This pest costs the country $230 million each year. The foxes prey on rabbits, helping a bit with the rabbit problem, but they also eat small farm animals like lambs, ducks, chickens and goats. Wildlife, especially animals that nest on the ground, are easy prey. But even tree-dwelling animals are not safe. In 2016, researchers discovered that sometimes foxes climb trees in search of baby koalas and squirrels.

Foxes threaten the critically endangered orange-bellied parrot.

Foxes have moved into urban environments.

Besides roaming the countryside, foxes are able to thrive in cities. There are rubbish bins to dig in, pet food dishes left on patios, and picnic scraps around parks and playgrounds. They hide under houses, in rock heaps and sometimes live in trees. They can carry diseases like distemper and mange that affect wildlife, working animals and family pets. Fox hunting is legal throughout Australia, and some states and cities have placed **bounties** on foxes, with hunters receiving $10 per fox **pelt**. Other methods of controlling the fox population include poison bait traps and reintroducing fox predators, like dingoes, or wild dogs, into the countryside. But the fox population continues to grow.

Australia's problem with rabbits and foxes is an example of how ordinary creatures, introduced on purpose into a new habitat, can become an invasive species.

CASE STUDY

Island invaders

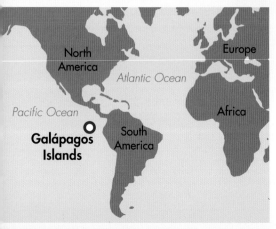

Islands are especially threatened by alien species. Because they are isolated by the surrounding waters, island plant and animal species develop with few strong competitors or predators. Invasive species introduced by humans into these ecosystems are the leading cause of extinction of native life.

One such group of islands is the Galápagos, off the Pacific coast of South America. They are the home of the giant tortoise. This magnificent creature can weigh over 180 kilograms and live for 100 or more years.

The Spanish discovered the islands and named them Galápagos, which meant "saddle", the shape of the tortoises' shells. Early settlers brought many alien species with them – some on purpose, like pigs, burros, cats, and plants such as vegetables and fruits. They brought others by accident, including rats, insects and weeds. It might be surprising, though, that the biggest threat of all these new visitors to the islands were the goats.

A giant Galápagos tortoise

Pigs

Burros

Cats

Rats

Insects

Plants and weeds

Since goats were introduced by whalers and pirates in the 1800s, wild herds have roamed the islands. By 1997, their numbers had grown to over 100,000.

The herds over-grazed the plants and grasses, causing a loss of the amazing **biodiversity** the islands had been known for. They even threatened the giant tortoises! You might wonder how that is possible.

A Galápagos tortoise at the Alcedo Volcano

Getting rid of the goats

The Alcedo Volcano is a gathering place for the tortoises during the cool, dry season. Dense, misty forests surround the rim of the volcano and provide shade and important drip pools where the tortoises rest – sometimes for 16 hours a day. The mists that drift up the slopes of the volcano become trapped by the trees and drip into the pools below. But when the goats invaded, they destroyed the forests. There was no longer any shade or a water supply for the tortoises, and the tortoises began to disappear.

To save the delicate ecosystem and the giant tortoises, Project Isabella began in 2000. Its main goal was the complete elimination of the **feral** goat herds. Trained sharpshooters in helicopters searched the island for goats and shot them. Some people were opposed to this large-scale slaughter of goats. However, the decision was made that the Galápagos ecosystem, under threat and found nowhere else on Earth, was valuable enough to justify their actions.

Very quickly, 90 per cent of the goat population was destroyed. The remaining goats grew wary of the hunters and began to hide high in the hills. The team had to come up with a new plan. They captured some goats and **sterilised** them so they could not reproduce. They fitted the goats with radio collars, then they released them. Because goats are herd animals, they went off to find other goats. With the radio collars, the hunters were able to track them and kill all the remaining animals. Project Isabella, completed in 2006, was the largest feral goat eradication project in the world.

Hunters in helicopters searched for the goats.

Did it work? Scientists and park rangers have been astounded at how quickly the plant life on the island has rebounded. The entire ecosystem is on the mend. Galápagos tortoise populations have grown from 3,000 to 19,000, but they are still considered endangered.

Saving the tortoise

Thanks to hard work by the Galápagos Conservancy, with support from a team of international conservation scientists, populations of giant tortoises are on the road to recovery.

The Giant Tortoise Restoration Initiative restores tortoise populations and, importantly, protects the ecosystems that are home to these incredible creatures.

This special conservation program has a long-term goal to help increase tortoise populations on the many islands that make up the Galápagos region.

It is a huge effort that is made up of four key parts.

1 Research and conservation for tortoises and the vegetation they need to survive.

2 Breeding and rearing tortoises of threatened species.

3 Repopulation of islands where tortoises were previously extinct.

4 Research and management of interactions between tortoises and humans.

A conservation success story

In the early 1960s, the Española tortoise population on the southern island of Española had dropped to just 15. Since conservation park guards brought those 15 into captivity, a breeding program has produced more than 2,000 offspring, which have now been released back onto their native island, along with the original 15 survivors. This conservation success story proves that threats to extinction can be halted – and reversed – with the right planning and care.

Breeding tortoises in captivity

The threat of humans

From the first time humans encountered these incredible animals, the future of the giant tortoise of the Galápagos Islands has been at risk.

The earliest visitors to the region were Spanish sailors, who caught them for food. Whalers were another threat to the population, with giant tortoises hunted in large numbers for food and as a source of oil.

As humans continued to explore the Galápagos region, they brought other threats with them, such as dogs, cats, rats, pigs and goats. These introduced species ate the eggs of the giant tortoise and also ate the vegetation that protected and nourished the ancient reptiles.

Today, although humans are largely responsible for the historical threats to the giant tortoise species, they are also responsible for positive conservation programs that help restore the population. At the same time, tourists visiting the Galápagos Islands continue to pose a risk and must obey strict rules that protect the native habitat.

Without the threat of humans, giant tortoises can live for more than 100 years, and by working together to look after their world, we can ensure they survive as a species for many hundreds more.

Conclusion

Both scientists and ordinary people like you must work together to protect our environment. Learning about **alien** invaders such as kudzu, cane toads and rock snot helps you become aware of the danger **invasive species** represent. We must avoid foolish mistakes. We also need to remedy the problems that already exist, whether caused by human error or natural disaster.

Glossary

algae plant-like living things that can make their own food, mostly found in water

alien totally different from the usual things that live in a particular place

biodiversity the variety of plants and animals living in a habitat

bounties sums of money paid for killing or capturing animals

ecosystem everything in a particular environment, including living things, such as plants and animals, and non-living things, such as water and rocks

facility a place where a particular event or activity happens

feral returned to a wild state; no longer domesticated or tame

fibre a thin, strong, thread-like piece of a plant

flammable can be easily set on fire and can burn very quickly

germinating the process where a seed begins to grow into a seedling

invasive spreads or multiplies very quickly and takes over an area

larvae the young form of many insects that hatch from eggs and turn into a very different form as an adult

microscopic so small that it can only be seen through a microscope

native a living thing that originated in the place where it continues to live

pelt an animal's skin with the fur on it

pupae insects that are in the process of turning into their adult forms

regenerate to grow again

repel to drive or force something away

species a group of living things that are alike in many ways, have many traits in common and are able to have offspring

sterilised made incapable of producing offspring

toxin a poison that is made by a living thing

Index